the

gardening

chantal marie

the importance of gardening

chantal marie

this book is for you

for her

and

for me too

the importance of gardening

chantal marie

contents

the importance of gardening

part one

she was baby blue

steady hands in between landscapes of wheat

newly trimmed white railings stretched until the side

the lawn freshly trimmed when the weather allowed

freshly carved birdhouse empty sprouts weeds

remains tucked under soil tended to regularly

her favorite past time at one point but no longer

where everything changed

remained very much the same

she asked if i could help her again

i told her i was sick at 10

    what a shame

i asked if she could help me

    i can't i have plans with shan

    you know she's my favorite out of you two

i told her i knew

i was sorry i asked

few more seasons of spring she was gone

bare beaten to death

uncle was trying to kill himself

she whispered to me on the phone

    now that shanny is gone

    you know you're my favorite don't you little bird?

i told her that yes

i knew

the first man of your life

broke you

looking for what you did not have

in every man since

everywhere

for the arms that are safe

to be held

you look just like her

is what they tell me

i suppose i do

we have the same blue eyes

raven hair, small frame

but we are very different

i am the stronger version of herself

she never knew

the importance of gardening

night time hung high

cups of whiskey

when my body did not belong to me

he held and pinned with selfish desperation

his eyes held the same black hatred

of his father's

he grabbed, groped, and gutted

until even i couldn't plead for him to stop anymore

and i stayed there alone

calling for help only long after he had left

had shut the door

it was your fault - he says

you did this - he says

you're just a waste of my time - he says

one year later she cried for me

knowing

she would have saved me - she says

if only she knew - she says

but i wished i could have saved myself

i felt anything but whole

on that cold cement floor

and i still remember the sound of his laugh

how unholy

just like his father who beat him and his mother

at 11:30

the importance of gardening

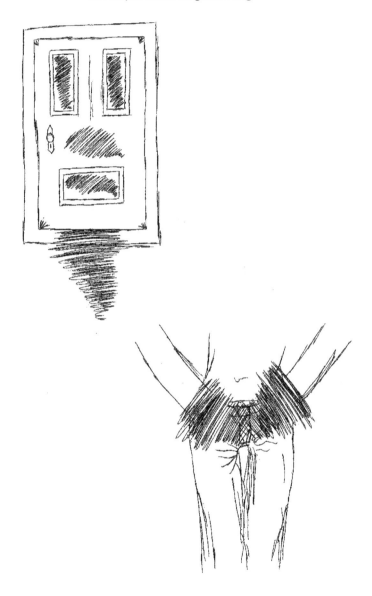

chantal marie

the importance of gardening

he told me it was my fault

that i deserved this

i heard it so often

i started to believe it

give me someone whose touch will ease

someone i can trust

someone who is different

because i have not been

that lucky

the importance of gardening

they call me a liar

he wishes i would

get over it already

no one is ever going to want you like this

<u>fathers and daughters</u>

how do you look with hope?

to see the universe

at firm planted feet?

and not a reminder

of what was failed

what has hurt

love seeping black tar

sickness etched onto my heart

our cycle

he tried to run from it too

i know

i'm having trouble letting it go

all those photos burnt

so long ago

the importance of gardening

sunday calls

i am not sure anymore

now that i've left

i'm trying, i am

what do i do? tell me please

i care, i do

but empty silence still hangs

conversations of chaos weather

have proven to get the best of me

this time

a loss of words

the familiarity and complexity of charred ends

i wish weren't

for things to be different, for broken to mend

for what never was to be

and i will talk to you same time,

next week

the importance of gardening

our usual,

you saying   *hello*

me saying   *hi*

and then silence

still small talk

staring at the clock

because neither one of us

knows what to say

to each other after everything

anymore

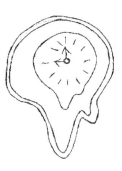

this love hurts

even though

it is not supposed to

you will be there with me

a reminder

of what not to do

the importance of gardening

what i wanted

someone to prove
to me they cared
someone to teach me
how safe feels

chantal marie

to those who were not brave enough

to raise with love and trust

for us

the importance of gardening

i am not sure if i would even be able to recognize

the things i need from a man

if they would be directly presented

in front of me

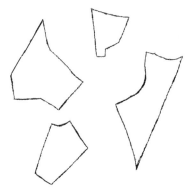

sunday school

weekdays time spent

i asked him, my broken self

begging for help

everything i did

for you, for them, for "me"

and i needed you

but i don't pray anymore

you shouldn't have made

me an atheist

the importance of gardening

i see the look in her eyes

when she tells me of the men

she had wished for instead

but she just turned eighteen

they screamed rehab

i wasn't sure if that would help me

why are you doing this

the taste of spit and bloody bodies

the smell of gasoline

your skin is turning green

after everything i'm alive

and lucky to be

the importance of gardening

a disease of generations

consuming descent

family

<u>nana</u>

slight careful steps

early morning hours

holding onto the railing

descending again into unpleasant things

the door remained stained

as everything else often did

little bird come in

swinging door pushing with might

atop the soft feathers she sat

bluejay she said

feather with flight, feather might

spent stories of mornings with carriages

and swishing tales

of the valley and daily sales

the importance of gardening

some did not so much understand

things are getting bad again

     little bird everything is going to be alright

     things get bad for me too

i am afraid to tell someone

     i know but i am here

     and when the days are dark, this is what you must do

     remember little bird

     when that does not work

     i will always be here

     to hold you

i can't wait to buy it

someday

     i can't wait to tell them

she used to say

i don't call her like i used to

she cannot read anymore

nor does she remember my name most days

the importance of gardening

part two

the importance of gardening

<u>home</u>

i have been looking
for years to find
to see and feel
the way safe would

i believed to have found it
had felt it
lying next to you

if i believed in a love at firsts

a love of that sort

i think it would have looked

something like you

the importance of gardening

you were nothing to me

i didn't think much of you

until i loved you

that was when you became everything

i let him believe

that i hated him

because i have trouble finding

the right words

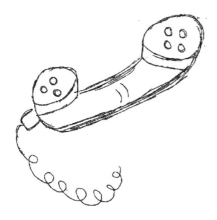

the importance of gardening

<u>for him</u>

thank you

for sticking by me

when i did not deserve it

all i want is to

see you

i just want to be close

to you

and i think i could be the one

for you

if you'll let me

the importance of gardening

i wish i knew

what came to mind

the moment you hear my name

i don't care how much

you may think your love difficult

because so is mine

and i'm willing to try

he was every hope

i ever had

if only we could have had

each other a little while longer

we began in love

let us end in it too

i still think of you

the importance of gardening

i close my eyes with thoughts of him

and wake with them too

maybe this is love

because everything comes back to you

we met in the middle of my mess

things could be different

this time

i think

the importance of gardening

mental health

past paths

threatening vines

pulling us back

i wish you would have tried harder

to fight for me

the importance of gardening

trying to undo you

but god i still want you

vacant pit stops

it would be different

i thought

someone to stay

the first our hands met

counting losses

shaking it off

i think i always knew

you would not

the importance of gardening

i cried for days

my eyes stung and my ears rang

for weeks and months

i slept at noon just to see his face

he never heard me though

no matter how much

i wanted him too

chance will not bring

us back together

only we can do that

the importance of gardening

he left with no more than a second glance

perhaps it was time for me

to get a taste of what i had done

so many times before

if you love me

tell me

before it's too late

the importance of gardening

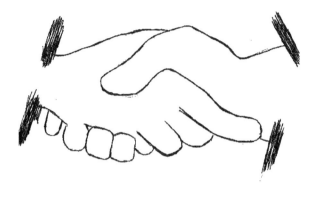

i'm wasting my time but

what if you and i were to have another chance?

my hope is that they do not compare

to me

that their hands do not fit

as nicely inside yours as mine did

shared the simple

that we did

i cannot stand to think about you

with someone else

the importance of gardening

certain days i am certain that you no longer reside

in the most kept places of my heart

finally this is it

but then i feel an empty ache

as soon as night time hangs high in the sky

when i am on a date with a sweet boy

i have decided to commit to someone new

and i don't want to move on, but perhaps it's time

still i find myself as time continues to pass

wishing for him, what could have been

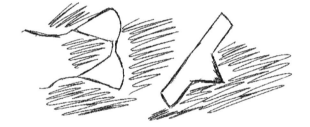

i am tired of them wanting my body

without making the effort to stay

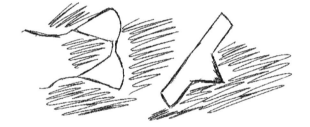

the importance of gardening

i cannot wait for you

i will not wait for you

but i would like you to know

that i want to

i am usually unable

to stay in one place for too long

 i would have

 stayed still though

 for you

the importance of gardening

when love comes let it

love is perfect in every way

it is we who are not

we are the ones

who make a mess out of it

part three

the importance of gardening

he felt sorry for himself

as he usually did

he cried for the things that broke him

that didn't exist

about me too

how i didn't care enough

i knew i didn't love him

as i watched him cry and thought

so what

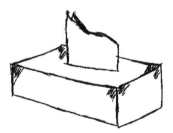

we walked at night, his footsteps light

hung shared mugs

the scent of newly picked sheets

he reached for my hand i had wished yours

like so many times before

we kissed and i felt gross

waiting –

to feel something other than you

something better than him

this was how it starts

losing what never was

i thought of leaving him that night

again

see you tomorrow

the importance of gardening

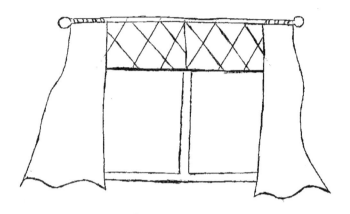

leaving was an escape

from them, this place

from it all

from me as well

sorry

he was confused i think

that every time we kissed

i wanted him

he was simply a way

to forget you

the importance of gardening

everyone leaves me

they want something other than gross obsession
he thinks equates love

i began to believe that it was
my fault again
that i did not want to be touched
at his convenience

i wanted better like the rest of them
so i left too

many nights i had spent

laying next to –

wondering if this was all there was

for me

waking at three

feeling as empty as i had at 11:30

seventeen

wrapped arms keys in hand

ready to leave

always been able to take care of myself

you were never my first choice

when i told you i loved you

i was lying

i am still sorry for this

for all of it

the importance of gardening

i tell them i will leave someday

that i have trouble feeling the way

they would like me too

they like the fire i carry

so they wait

but they do not listen

i see them

they all cry when i leave

wishing i hadn't

i have the constant need to leave

i am trying to learn

how to stay

the importance of gardening

naked bodies touched

by the wrong people

and i still do not know

what making love feels like

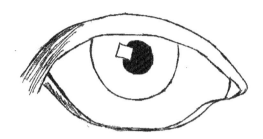

i see the way they don't look at each other

the way i would like someone

to look at me

the importance of gardening

i come with no instructions

on most days even i do not know

how to be

it is easy to love the idea

of me

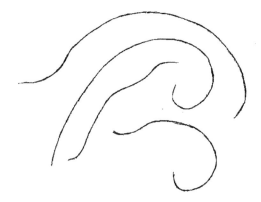

i met someone new

he had the same smirk and gentle eyes

though he didn't quite look at me the same way

as you

the importance of gardening

i wish he were here

sweet whispers

gentle touch

i only knew briefly

once

i wanted him to save me from

everything i couldn't see

including me

the importance of gardening

<u>lies i tell myself</u>

often things do not happen

at the right time

everything has its way

of working out

part four

the importance of gardening

we forget how it stays with us

even as we grow

i have only recently realized

that i placed myself

in the care of men

who would hurt

what i knew

they looked so much like you

you are still art

when he no longer admires

if he leaves

even when he changes his mind

the importance of gardening

at times i am afraid

of my writing

of the life this will make

the people it will hurt

<u>small towns</u>

for the old man who walks to the corner store
every day at 3

the elderly women who spend their time
baking sweet treats for that same small church
down the street just to fill their lonely

for the store owner's daughter who takes a seat
outside her father's shop like clockwork
at 11 and 2
wishing she could have been someone else
somewhere else

the importance of gardening

for the people who grew up and grew old
with kids of their own
who still spend their friday nights at the old hotel
at the end of main street
talks of crops and that one time in high school
still ring on their lips
frozen at seventeen

the kids with their bikes
who ride chasing the night

for the high school seniors sitting in class
two minutes away from it
college brochures clinging to fingertips

and for all the people here
in this small world you go overlooked
for me and for you

the importance of gardening

they think that they are not enough

i wish they could see the way they reflect

their effect

they do not see what i see

the importance of gardening

do not settle for someone

who does not respect you

in every way

these are the mistakes i have made

some days i feel as if i'm not doing enough

not working enough

not experiencing enough

whenever i feel like this i try

to remind myself that life cannot be

fulfilling all of the time

the importance of gardening

as i have gotten older, i have grown to let go
do not be afraid to let go of the past, of old friends, or places
figure out what fits in your life and what does not
this is what growing feels like

once i left

i thought things were

to be better there

that i would feel different

finally whole

perhaps it is not where we are

our outlook maybe

the importance of gardening

i am not sure

whether this process has

helped heal or destroy

it all feels the same

lost friends

i am not frightened to leave

or afraid to be alone

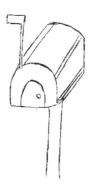

bodies our own

to belong to

and no one else

someday

i am trying to be content

often i long for more

to not be so still at times

even though i am quite far from that

tired towns where i have spent most of my life

leaving me on the verge of flight

most of the time

maybe if i keep moving i will find that one place

the place in my head that speaks home to me

where i no longer look

for more

the importance of gardening

to see more, to feel more

to look out *this is it*

it will all be worth it

when i find

it

maybe,

but i have been many places

and i have not found it

though i still dream of it

through the many years

i held myself

needing no one else

only wanting now

the importance of gardening

aches most days

that i must leave soon

to escape

so i can breathe

arms

strong enough to carry

hearts

large enough to heal

the importance of gardening

our lives spent

trying to be heard

over men who believe themselves

to be superior

your silence will hurt you

so much more

in the end

a place where my heart

would no longer need

the comfort

this is my idea of home

the importance of gardening

how do you remember while trying

to let go?

nothing is too great for you to achieve

you will hear differently

but people love to lie when they are afraid

the importance of gardening

there are days when i am fine
and days where i can't see the end of it

growing older
self-care has taught me how
to control my anxieties

to break free of whatever has hold on you

think of it

but only for a moment

let go

we all have a war inside of us

it is what drives us

what breaks us

i grew so much stronger

when i decided to accept

the apologies i didn't receive

but should have

the importance of gardening

when it consumes me i tell myself

if he had wanted to be with me

he would have

i am far from perfect

i have been hurt

i too, have done plenty of hurting

the importance of gardening

i am trying to be more gentle

despite what i've been given

in spite of everything that

has happened

forgiveness for the people

the events

that have hurt you

i am trying

to forgive it all

the things you do with your spare time

are important not frivolous

these are integral parts of our being

what we live for

do whatever you feel is best

that is enough

it has to be

the importance of gardening

at times it frightens me

how easily i seem

to fall back into

the life

the small world

that i have tried so hard

to run from

choose to be happy

to move on

we lose many things

but find ourselves

the importance of gardening

you are so much stronger

than you think,

you are capable

i would have liked to have gone back

to tell myself that

i was so busy wondering where he was

to save me that i had forgotten to save myself

the importance of gardening

words are so important to me

yet often i say the wrong thing
entirely

our love made a sweet story

perhaps that was all

it was meant to be

the importance of gardening

safe arms with strong hands

gentle enough for me

to fall into

this

is what saves me from it all

how i make it feel alright

the importance of gardening

thank you

for giving me

the voice to write

you've made it. thank you, so much.

i am so grateful for every single one of you.

this book was for you, as much as it was for me.

you have purchased a piece of me.

i am beyond grateful for my friends. they have supported me immensely throughout this journey.

they have encouraged me, and provided me with a safe space to write.

i wrote this book as a release for myself, hopeful that it would help heal.

the words i have trouble saying, what i run from at times.

i hope that this has been a comfort to you as well. that this provides a safe space of healing and understanding.

that is all i've ever really wanted.

truly, thank you.

about the writer:

chantal marie is a writer based in winnipeg, canada.

she has been writing from a young age, winning local competitions. studying literature and creative writing in post-secondary.

her writing includes themes of trauma, femininity, mental health, love, and loss.

when she is not writing, she spends her time travelling, and caring for animals.

you can find more of her at:

chantalmarie.org

as well as her social media:

http://www.instagram.com/chantalmarie.s

about the book:

the importance of gardening is a collection of poetry that focuses on,

trauma, femininity, mental health, love, and loss

the book is split into four parts. each part targeting a different stage of life.

a journey throughout. coming to terms with it, growing with it, and healing it.

CPSIA information can be obtained
at www.ICGtesting.com
Printed in the USA
LVOW13s1616221216
518439LV00029B/789/P